Zen as F*ck

BELONGS TO:

∙∙∙∙∙∙∙∙∙∙∙∙∙∙∙∙∙∙∙∙∙∙∙∙∙∙∙∙∙∙∙∙∙

5 Minutes a Day
to Cultivate
F*cking Gratitude, Mindfulness
and
Productivity

Shit I'm going to get done over the next 90 days?

_____
_____
_____
_____
_____
_____
_____
_____
_____
_____

How am I going to become more awesome?

_____
_____
_____
_____
_____
_____
_____

THIS MONTHS PLAN

My goals for month 1? (if I'm not too lazy)

'Believe you can and you're halfway there'
Theodore Roosevelt

What shit do I need to improve?

Something fun, crazy, or wild I will do this Month?

Date __/__/__

TODAY I AM F*UCKING THANKFUL FOR

1.
2.
3.

TODAY I FEEL : :) :| :(

How will I make today f*cking awesome ?

"The only thing that is ultimately real about your journey is the step that you are taking at this moment. That's all there ever is."
- **Sylvia Boorstein**

Todays moments that made me feel amazing

How could I have done sh*t today better

1 Simple goal for tomorrow

Date
___/___/___

TODAY I AM F*UCKING THANKFUL FOR

1. _____
2. _____
3. _____

TODAY I FEEL : 😊   😐   ☹️

How will I make today f*cking awesome ?

_____
_____
_____

"Meditation is to be aware of what is going on: in your body, in your feelings, in your mind, and in the world."
- Eckhart Tolle

Todays moments that made me feel great

_____
_____

How could I have done sh*t today better

_____
_____

1 Simple goal for tomorrow

_____

Date ___/___/___

TODAY I AM F*UCKING THANKFUL FOR

1. _____
2. _____
3. _____

TODAY I FEEL : ☺ 😐 ☹

How will I make today f*cking awesome ?

_____
_____
_____

"Mindfulness isn't difficult, we just need to remember to do it."
- Sharon Salzberg

Todays moments that made me feel amazing

_____
_____

How could I have done sh*t today better

_____
_____

1 Simple goal for tomorrow

_____

Date __/__/__

TODAY I AM F*UCKING THANKFUL FOR

1.
2.
3.

TODAY I FEEL : :) :| :(

How will I make today f*cking awesome ?

"Walk as if you are kissing the Earth with your feet."
- Thich Nhat Hanh

Todays moments that made me feel great

How could I have done sh*t today better

1 Simple goal for tomorrow

Date / /

TODAY I AM F*UCKING THANKFUL FOR

1.
2.
3.

TODAY I FEEL : :)   :| :(

How will I make today f*cking awesome ?

"Every time we become aware of a thought, as opposed to being lost in a thought, we experience that opening of the mind."
- Joseph Goldstein

Todays moments that made me feel amazing

How could I have done sh*t today better

1 Simple goal for tomorrow

Date ___/___/___

TODAY I AM F*UCKING THANKFUL FOR

1.
2.
3.

TODAY I FEEL : 😊 😐 ☹

How will I make today f*cking awesome ?

"Feelings come and go like clouds in a windy sky. Conscious breathing is my anchor."
- Thich Nhat Hanh

Todays moments that made me feel great

How could I have done sh*t today better

1 Simple goal for tomorrow

Date __/__/__

TODAY I AM F*UCKING THANKFUL FOR

1. ___
2. ___
3. ___

TODAY I FEEL : :)   :| :(

How will I make today f*cking awesome ?

___
___
___

"The greatest communication is usually how we are rather than what we say."
- Joseph Goldstein

Todays moments that made me feel amazing
___
___

How could I have done sh*t today better
___
___

1 Simple goal for tomorrow

Date __/__/__

TODAY I AM F*UCKING THANKFUL FOR

1.
2.
3.

TODAY I FEEL : 😊 😐 ☹

How will I make today f*cking awesome ?

"Wherever you are, be there totally."
- **Eckhart Tolle**

Todays moments that made me feel great

How could I have done sh*t today better

1 Simple goal for tomorrow

Date __/__/__

TODAY I AM F*UCKING THANKFUL FOR

1. _____
2. _____
3. _____

TODAY I FEEL :   :)   :| :(

How will I make today f*cking awesome ?

_____
_____
_____

"What you are looking for is what is looking."
- Joseph Goldstein

Todays moments that made me feel amazing

_____
_____

How could I have done sh*t today better

_____
_____

1 Simple goal for tomorrow

_____

Date ___/___/___

TODAY I AM F*UCKING THANKFUL FOR

1. _____
2. _____
3. _____

TODAY I FEEL : 😊 😐 ☹

How will I make today f*cking awesome ?

_____
_____
_____

"Do every act of your life as though it were the last act of your life."
- Marcus Aurelius

Todays moments that made me feel great

_____
_____

How could I have done sh*t today better

_____
_____

1 Simple goal for tomorrow

_____

Date __/__/__

TODAY I AM F*UCKING THANKFUL FOR

1. _____
2. _____
3. _____

TODAY I FEEL :   :)   :| :(

How will I make today f*cking awesome ?

_____
_____
_____

"If you miss the present moment, you miss your appointment with life. That is very serious!"
- Thich Nhat Hanh

Todays moments that made me feel amazing

_____
_____

How could I have done sh*t today better

_____
_____

1 Simple goal for tomorrow

_____

Date ___/___/___

TODAY I AM F*UCKING THANKFUL FOR

1.
2.
3.

TODAY I FEEL :   😊   😐   ☹

How will I make today f*cking awesome ?

"Meditate ... do not delay, lest you later regret it."
- The Buddha

Todays moments that made me feel great

How could I have done sh*t today better

1 Simple goal for tomorrow

Date __/__/__

TODAY I AM F*UCKING THANKFUL FOR

1. _____
2. _____
3. _____

TODAY I FEEL :   :)   :| :(

How will I make today f*cking awesome ?

_____
_____
_____

"Mindful and creative, a child who has neither a past, nor examples to follow, nor value judgments, simply lives, speaks and plays in freedom."
- Arnaud Desjardins

Todays moments that made me feel amazing

_____
_____

How could I have done sh*t today better

_____
_____

1 Simple goal for tomorrow

_____

Date ___/___/___

TODAY I AM F*UCKING THANKFUL FOR

1.
2.
3.

TODAY I FEEL : :)   :| :(

How will I make today f*cking awesome ?

"You can't stop the waves, but you can learn to surf."
- Jon Kabat-Zinn

Todays moments that made me feel great

How could I have done sh*t today better

1 Simple goal for tomorrow

Date __/__/__

TODAY I AM F*UCKING THANKFUL FOR

1. _____
2. _____
3. _____

TODAY I FEEL :   ☺   😐   ☹

How will I make today f*cking awesome ?

_____
_____
_____

"Until we can manage time, we can manage nothing else."
Peter Drucker

Todays moments that made me feel amazing

_____
_____

How could I have done sh*t today better

_____
_____

1 Simple goal for tomorrow

_____

Date __/__/__

TODAY I AM F*UCKING THANKFUL FOR

1.
2.
3.

TODAY I FEEL : 😊 😐 ☹

How will I make today f*cking awesome ?

"Amateurs sit and wait for inspiration, the rest of us just get up and go to work."
Stephen King

Todays moments that made me feel great

How could I have done sh*t today better

1 Simple goal for tomorrow

Date
/   /

TODAY I AM F*UCKING THANKFUL FOR

1. _____
2. _____
3. _____

TODAY I FEEL :   :)   :| :(

How will I make today f*cking awesome ?

_____
_____
_____

"If you spend too much time thinking about a thing, you'll never get it done."
Bruce Lee

Todays moments that made me feel amazing
_____
_____

How could I have done sh*t today better
_____
_____

1 Simple goal for tomorrow
_____

Date
___/___/___

TODAY I AM F*UCKING THANKFUL FOR

1. _____
2. _____
3. _____

TODAY I FEEL :   :)   :| :(

How will I make today f*cking awesome ?

_____
_____
_____

"It's not knowing what to do, it's doing what you know."
Tony Robbins

Todays moments that made me feel great

_____
_____

How could I have done sh*t today better

_____
_____

1 Simple goal for tomorrow

Date __/__/__

TODAY I AM F*UCKING THANKFUL FOR

1. _____
2. _____
3. _____

TODAY I FEEL : :)   :| :(

How will I make today f*cking awesome ?

_____
_____
_____

"When you do something, you should burn yourself up completely, like a good bonfire, leaving no trace of yourself."
- Shunryu Suzuki

Todays moments that made me feel amazing

_____
_____

How could I have done sh*t today better

_____
_____

1 Simple goal for tomorrow

_____

Date / /

TODAY I AM F*UCKING THANKFUL FOR

1.
2.
3.

TODAY I FEEL :   😊   😐   ☹️

How will I make today f*cking awesome ?

"Practice is this life, and realization is this life, and this life is revealed right here and now."
- Maezumi Roshi

Todays moments that made me feel great

How could I have done sh*t today better

1 Simple goal for tomorrow

Date ___/___/___

TODAY I AM F*UCKING THANKFUL FOR

1.
2.
3.

TODAY I FEEL : 😊 😐 ☹️

How will I make today f*cking awesome?

"Emotion arises at the place where mind & body meet. It is the body's reaction to mind."
- Eckhart Tolle

Todays moments that made me feel amazing

How could I have done sh*t today better

1 Simple goal for tomorrow

Date __/__/__

TODAY I AM F*UCKING THANKFUL FOR

1. _____
2. _____
3. _____

TODAY I FEEL :   ☺   😐   ☹

How will I make today f*cking awesome ?

_____
_____
_____

"Use every distraction as an object of meditation and they cease to be distractions."
- Mingyur Rinpoche

Todays moments that made me feel great

_____
_____

How could I have done sh*t today better

_____
_____

1 Simple goal for tomorrow

_____

Date __/__/__

TODAY I AM F*UCKING THANKFUL FOR

1. _____
2. _____
3. _____

TODAY I FEEL : 😊 😐 ☹️

How will I make today f*cking awesome ?

_____
_____
_____

"Happiness is your nature. It is not wrong to desire it. What is wrong is seeking it outside when it is inside."
- Ramana Maharshi

Todays moments that made me feel amazing

_____
_____

How could I have done sh*t today better

_____
_____

1 Simple goal for tomorrow

_____

Date __/__/__

TODAY I AM F*UCKING THANKFUL FOR

1.
2.
3.

TODAY I FEEL : 😊 😐 ☹

How will I make today f*cking awesome ?

"Ardently do today what must be done. Who knows? Tomorrow, death comes."
- The Buddha

Todays moments that made me feel great

How could I have done sh*t today better

1 Simple goal for tomorrow

Date / /

TODAY I AM F*UCKING THANKFUL FOR

1. _____
2. _____
3. _____

TODAY I FEEL :   😊   😐   ☹

How will I make today f*cking awesome ?

_____
_____
_____

"Your vision will become clear only when you look into your heart. Who looks outside, dreams. Who looks inside, awakens."
- Carl Jung

Todays moments that made me feel amazing

_____
_____

How could I have done sh*t today better

_____
_____

1 Simple goal for tomorrow

_____

Date __/__/__

TODAY I AM F*UCKING THANKFUL FOR

1.
2.
3.

TODAY I FEEL : 😊 😐 ☹

How will I make today f*cking awesome ?

"Awareness is the greatest agent for change."
- Eckhart Tolle

Todays moments that made me feel great

How could I have done sh*t today better

1 Simple goal for tomorrow

Date __/__/__

TODAY I AM F*UCKING THANKFUL FOR

1.
2.
3.

TODAY I FEEL : :) :| :(

How will I make today f*cking awesome ?

"Reality is only an agreement - today is always today."
- Zen Proverb

Todays moments that made me feel amazing

How could I have done sh*t today better

1 Simple goal for tomorrow

Date __/__/__

TODAY I AM F*UCKING THANKFUL FOR

1.
2.
3.

TODAY I FEEL : 😊   😐   ☹

How will I make today f*cking awesome ?

"The significance is hiding in the insignificant. Appreciate everything."
- Eckhart Tolle

Todays moments that made me feel great

How could I have done sh*t today better

1 Simple goal for tomorrow

Date __/__/____

TODAY I AM F*UCKING THANKFUL FOR

1. _____
2. _____
3. _____

TODAY I FEEL : :)   :| :(

How will I make today fucking awesome ?

_____
_____
_____

"Train yourself never to put off the word or action for the expression of gratitude." – Albert Schweitzer

Todays moments that made me feel great

_____
_____

How could I have made today better

_____
_____

1 Simple goal for tomorrow

_____

Date ___/___/___

TODAY I AM F*UCKING THANKFUL FOR

1. ___
2. ___
3. ___

TODAY I FEEL : 😊 😐 ☹️

How will I make today fucking awesome ?

___
___
___

"Train yourself never to put off the word or action for the expression of gratitude." – Albert Schweitzer

Todays moments that made me feel great

___
___

How could I have made today better

___
___

1 Simple goal for tomorrow

___

Shit I'm going to get done over the next 90 days?

_____
_____
_____
_____
_____
_____
_____
_____
_____
_____
_____

How am I going to become more awesome?

_____
_____
_____
_____
_____
_____
_____

THIS MONTHS PLAN

My goals for month 1? (if I'm not too lazy)

___

'Believe you can and you're halfway there'
Theodore Roosevelt

What shit do I need to improve?

___

Something fun, crazy, or wild I will do this Month?

Date __/__/__

TODAY I AM F*UCKING THANKFUL FOR

1. _____
2. _____
3. _____

TODAY I FEEL :   :)   :| :(

How will I make today f*cking awesome ?

_____
_____
_____

"It is not enough to be busy... The question is: what are we busy about?"
Henry David Thoreau

Todays moments that made me feel amazing

_____
_____

How could I have done sh*t today better

_____
_____

1 Simple goal for tomorrow

_____

Date / /

TODAY I AM F*UCKING THANKFUL FOR

1.
2.
3.

TODAY I FEEL :

How will I make today f*cking awesome ?

"Your mind is for having ideas, not holding them."
David Allen

Todays moments that made me feel great

How could I have done sh*t today better

1 Simple goal for tomorrow

Date __/__/__

TODAY I AM F*UCKING THANKFUL FOR

1. _____
2. _____
3. _____

TODAY I FEEL : 😊 😐 ☹

How will I make today f*cking awesome ?

_____
_____
_____

> "Nothing is less productive than to make more efficient what should not be done at all."
> **Peter Drucker**

Todays moments that made me feel amazing

_____
_____

How could I have done sh*t today better

_____
_____

1 Simple goal for tomorrow

_____

Date ___/___/___

TODAY I AM F*UCKING THANKFUL FOR

1. _____
2. _____
3. _____

TODAY I FEEL : 😊 😐 ☹

How will I make today f*cking awesome ?

_____
_____
_____

"Success is often achieved by those who don't know that failure is inevitable."
Coco Chanel

Todays moments that made me feel great

_____
_____

How could I have done sh*t today better

_____
_____

1 Simple goal for tomorrow

_____

Date / /

TODAY I AM F*UCKING THANKFUL FOR

1.
2.
3.

TODAY I FEEL : :) :| :(

How will I make today f*cking awesome ?

"We have only now, only this single eternal moment opening and unfolding before us, day and night."
Jack Kornfield

Todays moments that made me feel amazing

How could I have done sh*t today better

1 Simple goal for tomorrow

Date ___/___/___

TODAY I AM F*UCKING THANKFUL FOR

1. _____
2. _____
3. _____

TODAY I FEEL : 🙂 😐 ☹️

How will I make today f*cking awesome ?

_____
_____
_____

"Perfection of character is this: to live each day as if it were your last, without frenzy, without apathy, without pretense."
- Marcus Aurelius, Meditations

Todays moments that made me feel great

_____
_____

How could I have done sh*t today better

_____
_____

1 Simple goal for tomorrow

_____

Date ___/___/___

TODAY I AM F*UCKING THANKFUL FOR

1. _____
2. _____
3. _____

TODAY I FEEL : 😊 😐 ☹️

How will I make today f*cking awesome ?

_____
_____
_____

"Guilt, regret, resentment, sadness & all forms of nonforgiveness are caused by too much past & not enough presence."
- Eckhart Tolle

Todays moments that made me feel amazing

_____
_____

How could I have done sh*t today better

_____
_____

1 Simple goal for tomorrow

_____

Date ___/___/___

TODAY I AM F*UCKING THANKFUL FOR

1.
2.
3.

TODAY I FEEL :   :)   :| :(

How will I make today f*cking awesome ?

"Mindfulness, the Root of Happiness"
- **Joseph Goldstein**

Todays moments that made me feel great

How could I have done sh*t today better

1 Simple goal for tomorrow

Date ___/___/___

TODAY I AM F*UCKING THANKFUL FOR

1. _____
2. _____
3. _____

TODAY I FEEL : :)   :| :(

How will I make today f*cking awesome ?

_____
_____
_____

"The real voyage of discovery consists not in seeking out new landscapes but in having new eyes."
- Marcel Proust

Todays moments that made me feel amazing

_____
_____

How could I have done sh*t today better

_____
_____

1 Simple goal for tomorrow

_____

Date __/__/__

TODAY I AM F*UCKING THANKFUL FOR

1.
2.
3.

TODAY I FEEL : :) :| :(

How will I make today f*cking awesome ?

"The key is not to prioritize what's on your schedule, but to schedule your priorities."
Stephen Covey

Todays moments that made me feel great

How could I have done sh*t today better

1 Simple goal for tomorrow

Date ___/___/___

TODAY I AM F*UCKING THANKFUL FOR

1. _____
2. _____
3. _____

TODAY I FEEL :   :)   :| :(

How will I make today f*cking awesome ?

_____
_____
_____

> "Ordinary people think merely of spending time, great people think of using it."
> **Arthur Schopenhauer**

Todays moments that made me feel amazing

_____
_____

How could I have done sh*t today better

_____
_____

1 Simple goal for tomorrow

_____

Date ___/___/___

TODAY I AM F*UCKING THANKFUL FOR

1.
2.
3.

TODAY I FEEL :   😊   😐   ☹

How will I make today f*cking awesome ?

"Time is the scarcest resource and unless it is managed nothing else can be managed"
Peter Drucker

Todays moments that made me feel great

How could I have done sh*t today better

1 Simple goal for tomorrow

Date ___/___/___

TODAY I AM F*UCKING THANKFUL FOR

1. _____
2. _____
3. _____

TODAY I FEEL :   :)   :| :(

How will I make today f*cking awesome ?

_____
_____
_____

"Focus on being productive instead of busy."
Tim Ferriss

Todays moments that made me feel amazing

_____
_____

How could I have done sh*t today better

_____
_____

1 Simple goal for tomorrow

_____

Date __/__/__

TODAY I AM F*UCKING THANKFUL FOR

1. _____
2. _____
3. _____

TODAY I FEEL : ☺ 😐 ☹

How will I make today f*cking awesome ?

_____
_____
_____

"Time is at once the most valuable and the most perishable of all our possessions"
John Randolph

Todays moments that made me feel great

_____
_____

How could I have done sh*t today better

_____
_____

1 Simple goal for tomorrow

_____

Date __/__/__

TODAY I AM F*UCKING THANKFUL FOR

1. _____
2. _____
3. _____

TODAY I FEEL : 😊 😐 ☹️

How will I make today f*cking awesome ?

_____
_____
_____

> "Absorb what is useful, reject what is useless, add what is specifically your own."
> **Bruce Lee**

Todays moments that made me feel amazing

_____
_____

How could I have done sh*t today better

_____
_____

1 Simple goal for tomorrow

_____

Date __/__/__

TODAY I AM F*UCKING THANKFUL FOR

1. _____
2. _____
3. _____

TODAY I FEEL : ☺ 😐 ☹

How will I make today f*cking awesome ?

_____
_____
_____
_____

"Efficiency is doing better what is already being done."
Peter Drucker

Todays moments that made me feel great

_____
_____

How could I have done sh*t today better

_____
_____

1 Simple goal for tomorrow

_____

Date __/__/__

TODAY I AM F*UCKING THANKFUL FOR

1.
2.
3.

TODAY I FEEL : 😊 😐 ☹

How will I make today f*cking awesome ?

"This is the real secret of life — to be completely engaged with what you are doing in the here and now. And instead of calling it work, realize it is play."-
Alan Watts

Todays moments that made me feel amazing

How could I have done sh*t today better

1 Simple goal for tomorrow

Date ___/___/___

TODAY I AM F*UCKING THANKFUL FOR

1. _____
2. _____
3. _____

TODAY I FEEL : :) :| :(

How will I make today f*cking awesome ?

_____
_____
_____

"The only way to live is by accepting each minute as an unrepeatable miracle."
- Tara Brach

Todays moments that made me feel great

_____
_____

How could I have done sh*t today better

_____
_____

1 Simple goal for tomorrow

_____

Date __/__/____

TODAY I AM F*UCKING THANKFUL FOR

1.
2.
3.

TODAY I FEEL : 🙂 😐 ☹️

How will I make today f*cking awesome ?

"Today, you can decide to walk in freedom. You can choose to walk differently. You can walk as a free person, enjoying every step."
- Thich Nhat Hanh

Todays moments that made me feel amazing

How could I have done sh*t today better

1 Simple goal for tomorrow

Date __/__/__

TODAY I AM F*UCKING THANKFUL FOR

1. _____
2. _____
3. _____

TODAY I FEEL : :)   :| :(

How will I make today f*cking awesome ?

_____
_____
_____

"In today's rush, we all think too much — seek too much — want too much — and forget about the joy of just being."
- **Eckhart Tolle**

Todays moments that made me feel great

_____
_____

How could I have done sh*t today better

_____
_____

1 Simple goal for tomorrow

_____

Date __/__/__

TODAY I AM F*UCKING THANKFUL FOR

1. _____
2. _____
3. _____

TODAY I FEEL :   😊   😐   ☹️

How will I make today f*cking awesome ?

_____
_____
_____

> "Life is not lost by dying; life is lost minute by minute, day by dragging day, in all the small uncaring ways."
> **- Stephen Vincent Benet**

Todays moments that made me feel amazing

_____
_____

How could I have done sh*t today better

_____
_____

1 Simple goal for tomorrow

_____

Date __/__/__

TODAY I AM F*UCKING THANKFUL FOR

1. _____
2. _____
3. _____

TODAY I FEEL : 😊 😐 ☹

How will I make today f*cking awesome ?

_____
_____
_____

"I feel that luck is preparation meeting opportunity."
Oprah Winfrey

Todays moments that made me feel great

_____
_____

How could I have done sh*t today better

_____
_____

1 Simple goal for tomorrow

Date __/__/__

TODAY I AM F*UCKING THANKFUL FOR

1. ___
2. ___
3. ___

TODAY I FEEL :   :)   :| :(

How will I make today f*cking awesome ?

___
___
___

"Effective performance is preceded by painstaking preparation"
Brian Tracy

Todays moments that made me feel amazing
___
___

How could I have done sh*t today better
___
___

1 Simple goal for tomorrow
___

Date __/__/__

TODAY I AM F*UCKING THANKFUL FOR

1. _____
2. _____
3. _____

TODAY I FEEL :   😊   😐   ☹️

How will I make today f*cking awesome ?

_____
_____

"The desire of knowledge, like the thirst for riches, increases ever with the acquisition of it."
Laurence Sterne

Todays moments that made me feel great

_____
_____

How could I have done sh*t today better

_____
_____

1 Simple goal for tomorrow

_____

Date / /

TODAY I AM F*UCKING THANKFUL FOR

1.
2.
3.

TODAY I FEEL : 🙂 😐 🙁

How will I make today f*cking awesome ?

"The great accomplishments of man have resulted from the transmission of ideas of enthusiasm."
Thomas J. Watson

Todays moments that made me feel amazing

How could I have done sh*t today better

1 Simple goal for tomorrow

Date
___/___/___

TODAY I AM F*UCKING THANKFUL FOR

1. _____
2. _____
3. _____

TODAY I FEEL :   :)   :| :(

How will I make today f*cking awesome ?

_____
_____
_____

"Don't confuse the urgent with the important."
Preston Ni

Todays moments that made me feel great

_____
_____

How could I have done sh*t today better

_____
_____

1 Simple goal for tomorrow

_____

Date
/ /

TODAY I AM F*UCKING THANKFUL FOR

1.
2.
3.

TODAY I FEEL :   :)   :| :(

How will I make today f*cking awesome ?

"What would it be like if I could accept life--accept this moment--exactly as it is?"
- **Tara Brach**

Todays moments that made me feel amazing

How could I have done sh*t today better

1 Simple goal for tomorrow

Date __/__/__

TODAY I AM F*UCKING THANKFUL FOR

1.
2.
3.

TODAY I FEEL : 😊 😐 ☹️

How will I make today f*cking awesome ?

"Everything is created twice, first in the mind and then in reality."
- Robin S. Sharma

Todays moments that made me feel great

How could I have done sh*t today better

1 Simple goal for tomorrow

Date __/__/__

TODAY I AM F*UCKING THANKFUL FOR

1.
2.
3.

TODAY I FEEL : 😊 😐 ☹

How will I make today f*cking awesome ?

> "Mindfulness, also called wise attention, helps us see what we're adding to our experiences, not only during meditation sessions but also elsewhere."
> **Sharon Salzberg**

Todays moments that made me feel amazing

How could I have done sh*t today better

1 Simple goal for tomorrow

Date __/__/__

TODAY I AM F*UCKING THANKFUL FOR

1.
2.
3.

TODAY I FEEL : 😊   😐   ☹

How will I make today f*cking awesome ?

"We use mindfulness to observe the way we cling to pleasant experiences & push away unpleasant ones."
Sharon Salzberg

Todays moments that made me feel great

How could I have done sh*t today better

1 Simple goal for tomorrow

Date __/__/__

TODAY I AM F*UCKING THANKFUL FOR

1. _____
2. _____
3. _____

TODAY I FEEL : ☺ 😐 ☹

How will I make today f*cking awesome ?

_____
_____
_____

"It's not about approving or liking, but just being able to allow the world to be the way it is without resenting, hating, or judging it."
- Buddhism Now

Todays moments that made me feel amazing

_____
_____

How could I have done sh*t today better

_____
_____

1 Simple goal for tomorrow

_____

Date
___/___/___

TODAY I AM F*UCKING THANKFUL FOR

1.
2.
3.

TODAY I FEEL : 😊 😐 ☹

How will I make today f*cking awesome ?

"When you are present, you can allow the mind to be as it is without getting entangled in it."
- **Eckhart Tolle**

Todays moments that made me feel great

How could I have done sh*t today better

1 Simple goal for tomorrow

Shit I'm going to get done over the next 90 days?

How am I going to become more awesome?

THIS MONTHS PLAN

My goals for month 1? (if I'm not too lazy)

How will I make today f*cking awesome ?

'Believe you can and you're halfway there'
Theodore Roosevelt

What shit do I need to improve?

How could I have done sh*t today better

Something fun, crazy, or wild I will do this Month?

Date __/__/____

TODAY I AM F*UCKING THANKFUL FOR

1.
2.
3.

TODAY I FEEL : 😊 😐 ☹️

How will I make today f*cking awesome ?

"We cannot be present and run our story-line at the same time."
Pema Chödrön

Todays moments that made me feel amazing

How could I have done sh*t today better

1 Simple goal for tomorrow

Date __/__/__

TODAY I AM F*UCKING THANKFUL FOR

1. _____
2. _____
3. _____

TODAY I FEEL : 🙂 😐 🙁

How will I make today f*cking awesome ?

_____
_____
_____

"Every problem perceived to be 'out there' is really nothing more than a misperception within your own thinking."
Byron Katie

Todays moments that made me feel great

_____
_____

How could I have done sh*t today better

_____
_____

1 Simple goal for tomorrow

Date __/__/__

TODAY I AM F*UCKING THANKFUL FOR

1.
2.
3.

TODAY I FEEL : :) :| :(

How will I make today f*cking awesome ?

"Both good and bad days should end with productivity. You mood affairs should never influence your work."
Greg Evans

Todays moments that made me feel amazing

How could I have done sh*t today better

1 Simple goal for tomorrow

Date
___/___/___

TODAY I AM F*UCKING THANKFUL FOR

1. _____
2. _____
3. _____

TODAY I FEEL :   😊   😐   ☹️

How will I make today f*cking awesome ?

_____
_____
_____

"Efficiency is doing things right. Effectiveness is doing the right things."
Peter Drucker

Todays moments that made me feel great

_____
_____

How could I have done sh*t today better

_____
_____

1 Simple goal for tomorrow

_____

Date ___/___/___

TODAY I AM F*UCKING THANKFUL FOR

1. _____
2. _____
3. _____

TODAY I FEEL : 😊 😐 ☹️

How will I make today f*cking awesome ?

_____
_____
_____

"You don't need a new plan for next year. You need a commitment."
Seth Godin

Todays moments that made me feel amazing
_____
_____

How could I have done sh*t today better
_____
_____

1 Simple goal for tomorrow

Date
___/___/___

TODAY I AM F*UCKING THANKFUL FOR

1. _____
2. _____
3. _____

TODAY I FEEL :   :)   :| :(

How will I make today f*cking awesome ?

_____
_____
_____

"To the degree we're not living our dreams; our comfort zone has more control of us than we have over ourselves."
Peter McWilliams

Todays moments that made me feel great

_____
_____

How could I have done sh*t today better

_____
_____

1 Simple goal for tomorrow

_____

Date / /

TODAY I AM F*UCKING THANKFUL FOR

1.
2.
3.

TODAY I FEEL : 😊 😐 ☹️

How will I make today f*cking awesome ?

"If there are nine rabbits on the ground, if you want to catch one, just focus on one."
Jack Ma

Todays moments that made me feel amazing

How could I have done sh*t today better

1 Simple goal for tomorrow

Date
/ /

TODAY I AM F*UCKING THANKFUL FOR

1.
2.
3.

TODAY I FEEL : ☺ 😐 ☹

How will I make today f*cking awesome ?

"When one has much to put into them, a day has a hundred pockets."
Friedrich Nietzsche

Todays moments that made me feel great

How could I have done sh*t today better

1 Simple goal for tomorrow

Date ___/___/___

TODAY I AM F*UCKING THANKFUL FOR

1. _____
2. _____
3. _____

TODAY I FEEL : 😊 😐 ☹️

How will I make today f*cking awesome ?

_____
_____
_____

"Surviving a failure gives you more self-confidence. Failures are great learning tools.. but they must be kept to a minimum."
Jeffrey Immelt

Todays moments that made me feel amazing
_____
_____

How could I have done sh*t today better
_____
_____

1 Simple goal for tomorrow
_____

Date ___/___/___

TODAY I AM F*UCKING THANKFUL FOR

1.
2.
3.

TODAY I FEEL :   :)   :| :(

How will I make today f*cking awesome ?

"A life spent making mistakes is not only more honorable, but more useful than a life spent doing nothing"
George Bernard Shaw

Todays moments that made me feel great

How could I have done sh*t today better

1 Simple goal for tomorrow

Date ___/___/___

TODAY I AM F*UCKING THANKFUL FOR

1.
2.
3.

TODAY I FEEL : 🙂 😐 🙁

How will I make today f*cking awesome ?

"Working on the right thing is probably more important than working hard."
Caterina Fake

Todays moments that made me feel amazing

How could I have done sh*t today better

1 Simple goal for tomorrow

Date ___/___/___

TODAY I AM F*UCKING THANKFUL FOR

1. _____
2. _____
3. _____

TODAY I FEEL : 🙂 😐 🙁

How will I make today f*cking awesome ?

_____
_____
_____

"Follow effective actions with quiet reflection. From the quiet reflection will come even more effective action."
Peter Drucker

Todays moments that made me feel great

_____
_____

How could I have done sh*t today better

_____
_____

1 Simple goal for tomorrow

_____

Date __/__/__

TODAY I AM F*UCKING THANKFUL FOR

1. _____
2. _____
3. _____

TODAY I FEEL : :) :| :(

How will I make today f*cking awesome ?
_____
_____
_____

"Few of us ever live in the present. We are forever anticipating what is to come or remembering what has gone."
Louis L'Amour

Todays moments that made me feel amazing
_____
_____

How could I have done sh*t today better
_____
_____

1 Simple goal for tomorrow
_____

Date __/__/__

TODAY I AM F*UCKING THANKFUL FOR

1.
2.
3.

TODAY I FEEL : :)   :| :(

How will I make today f*cking awesome ?

"If you want to conquer the anxiety of life, live in the moment, live in the breath."-
Amit Ray

Todays moments that made me feel great

How could I have done sh*t today better

1 Simple goal for tomorrow

Date ___/___/___

TODAY I AM F*UCKING THANKFUL FOR

1.
2.
3.

TODAY I FEEL :   :)   :| :(

How will I make today f*cking awesome ?

"If you aren't in the moment, you are either looking forward to uncertainty, or back to pain and regret."
Jim Carrey

Todays moments that made me feel amazing

How could I have done sh*t today better

1 Simple goal for tomorrow

Date ___/___/___

TODAY I AM F*UCKING THANKFUL FOR

1. _____
2. _____
3. _____

TODAY I FEEL : 😊 😐 ☹

How will I make today f*cking awesome ?

_____
_____
_____

"All beings want to be happy, yet so very few know how. It is out of ignorance that any of us cause suffering, for ourselves or for others"
- Sharon Salzberg

Todays moments that made me feel great

_____
_____

How could I have done sh*t today better

_____
_____

1 Simple goal for tomorrow

_____

Date ___/___/___

TODAY I AM F*UCKING THANKFUL FOR

1. _____
2. _____
3. _____

TODAY I FEEL : ☺ 😐 ☹

How will I make today f*cking awesome ?

_____
_____
_____

"The energy of mindfulness has the element of friendship and loving kindness in it."
- Thich Nhat Hanh

Todays moments that made me feel amazing
_____
_____

How could I have done sh*t today better
_____
_____

1 Simple goal for tomorrow
_____

Date ___/___/___

TODAY I AM F*UCKING THANKFUL FOR

1. _____
2. _____
3. _____

TODAY I FEEL : 😊   😐   ☹️

How will I make today f*cking awesome?

_____
_____
_____

"Look at other people and ask yourself if you are really seeing them or just your thoughts about them."
Jon Kabat-Zinn

Todays moments that made me feel great

_____
_____

How could I have done sh*t today better

_____
_____

1 Simple goal for tomorrow

_____

Date __/__/__

TODAY I AM F*UCKING THANKFUL FOR

1. _____
2. _____
3. _____

TODAY I FEEL : 😊   😐   ☹️

How will I make today f*cking awesome ?

_____
_____
_____

> "We often have very little empathy for our own thoughts and feelings and frequently try to suppress them by dismissing them as weaknesses."
> **- Mark Williams**

Todays moments that made me feel amazing

_____
_____

How could I have done sh*t today better

_____
_____

1 Simple goal for tomorrow

_____

Date __/__/__

TODAY I AM F*UCKING THANKFUL FOR

1.
2.
3.

TODAY I FEEL : :)   :| :(

How will I make today f*cking awesome ?

"The most precious gift we can offer others is our presence. When mindfulness embraces those we love, they will bloom like flowers."-
Thich Nhat Hanh

Todays moments that made me feel great

How could I have done sh*t today better

1 Simple goal for tomorrow

Date __/__/__

TODAY I AM F*UCKING THANKFUL FOR

1. _____
2. _____
3. _____

TODAY I FEEL : :)   :| :(

How will I make today f*cking awesome ?

_____
_____
_____

"There is no substitute for hard work."
Thomas Edison

Todays moments that made me feel amazing

_____
_____

How could I have done sh*t today better

_____
_____

1 Simple goal for tomorrow

_____

Date ___/___/___

TODAY I AM F*UCKING THANKFUL FOR

1. _____
2. _____
3. _____

TODAY I FEEL : 😊 😐 ☹

How will I make today f*cking awesome ?

_____
_____
_____

"Action is the foundational key to all success."
Picasso

Todays moments that made me feel great

_____
_____

How could I have done sh*t today better

_____
_____

1 Simple goal for tomorrow

_____

Date ___/___/___

TODAY I AM F*UCKING THANKFUL FOR

1.
2.
3.

TODAY I FEEL : 😊 😐 ☹️

How will I make today f*cking awesome ?

"Never mistake motion for action."
Ernest Hemingway

Todays moments that made me feel amazing

How could I have done sh*t today better

1 Simple goal for tomorrow

Date
___/___/___

TODAY I AM F*UCKING THANKFUL FOR

1. _____
2. _____
3. _____

TODAY I FEEL :   :)   :| :(

How will I make today f*cking awesome ?

_____
_____
_____

"While one person hesitates because he feels inferior, the other is busy making mistakes and becoming superior."
Henry Link

Todays moments that made me feel great

_____
_____

How could I have done sh*t today better

_____
_____

1 Simple goal for tomorrow

_____

Date / /

TODAY I AM F*UCKING THANKFUL FOR

1.
2.
3.

TODAY I FEEL :   :)   :| :(

How will I make today f*cking awesome ?

"No matter how great the talent or efforts, some things just take time. You can't produce a baby in one month by getting nine women pregnant."
Warren Buffett

Todays moments that made me feel amazing

How could I have done sh*t today better

1 Simple goal for tomorrow

Date __/__/__

TODAY I AM F*UCKING THANKFUL FOR

1. _____
2. _____
3. _____

TODAY I FEEL :   :)   :| :(

How will I make today f*cking awesome ?

_____
_____
_____

"My goal is no longer to get more done, but rather to have less to do."
Francine Jay

Todays moments that made me feel great

_____
_____

How could I have done sh*t today better

_____
_____

1 Simple goal for tomorrow

_____

Date __/__/__

TODAY I AM F*UCKING THANKFUL FOR

1. _____
2. _____
3. _____

TODAY I FEEL : 😊 😐 ☹️

How will I make today f*cking awesome ?

_____
_____
_____

"Improved productivity means less human sweat, not more."
Henry Ford

Todays moments that made me feel amazing
_____
_____

How could I have done sh*t today better
_____
_____

1 Simple goal for tomorrow
_____

Date ___/___/___

TODAY I AM F*UCKING THANKFUL FOR

1. _____
2. _____
3. _____

TODAY I FEEL : 😊 😐 ☹️

How will I make today f*cking awesome ?

_____
_____
_____

"The noblest search is the search for excellence."
Lyndon B. Johnson

Todays moments that made me feel great

_____
_____

How could I have done sh*t today better

_____
_____

1 Simple goal for tomorrow

_____

Date ___/___/___

TODAY I AM F*UCKING THANKFUL FOR

1. _____
2. _____
3. _____

TODAY I FEEL : 😊 😐 ☹

How will I make today f*cking awesome ?

_____
_____
_____

"It's not always that we need to do more but rather that we need to focus on less."
Nathan W. Morris

Todays moments that made me feel amazing

_____
_____

How could I have done sh*t today better

_____
_____

1 Simple goal for tomorrow

_____

Date __/__/__

TODAY I AM F*UCKING THANKFUL FOR

1. _____
2. _____
3. _____

TODAY I FEEL : 😊 😐 ☹️

How will I make today f*cking awesome ?

_____
_____
_____

"You must remain focused on your journey to greatness."
Les Brown

Todays moments that made me feel great

_____
_____

How could I have done sh*t today better

_____
_____

1 Simple goal for tomorrow

_____

Made in the USA
Middletown, DE
17 March 2022